STRIFE
AND
LIFE

MY PERFECTLY IMPERFECT LIFE'S

Journey

SONIA B. LEE

Foreword by

Bishop Dr. Philip H. London

Coral Springs, FL

Strife and Life: My Perfectly Imperfect Life's Journey
Copyright © 2021 Sonia Lee

ISBN: 979-8-9850280-0-3 (print)
ISBN: 979-8-9850280-1-0 (ebook)

Library of Congress Control Number: 2021949801

Cover design: Andre Pryce
Interior layout: Annette R. Johnson, Allwrite Communications

Printed in the United States of America

Dedication

This book is dedicated to the Holy Spirit, who inspired me to share my testimony. I would also like to dedicate this book to my five children, Dorrette, Natalee, Shae, Ann Marie and Kerlande, and my nine grandchildren, Elijah John, Elizabeth, Karter, Kimbella, Kymani, Nathan, David, and Zion. I also dedicate this book to my Heart of Compassion Ministries family who trust in my leadership and also allow me to be their mentor. It is not always easy keeping up with my dedication to the Lord's work but it is necessary.

Contents

Author's Note

Apostle John L. Mohorn Jr. is my spiritual father and Apostolic covering. He spoke in my life about the calling of God on my life 20 years ago. I am honored to have him in my life. His love, prayers, and encouragement are exceptional. I have never been the same in ministry since our destinies collided. Although he is mentioned in the book only briefly, his impact in my life has been enduring.

Acknowledgments

I want to express my gratitude Sister Nakeeta McNeil. She is my spiritual daughter who stood by me right throughout this entire publishing process. I pray for the favor of God to overtake your life.

My intercessor, Natalee Pryce, who is my biological daughter, you see and sense it all in the spiritual realm. Continue to pray for your mom. May your store basket never go empty.

To my son-in-law and cover designer of my book Elder Andre Pryce, the one who stood with me in ministry. I speak more than enough blessings in your life forever. Your labor will not be in vain.

Thank you to my dad and all of my siblings. I truly love you all.

I appreciate all of my colleagues in the Gospel, including Apostle Ruth Mobley, Bishop Walters and Pastor Sandra Walters, and Bishop London and Apostle Clothel London. Similarly, I express a special thank you to every ministry leader who spoke into or impacted my life over the years. I love you and God bless you.

And last but definitely not least, to the millions who will read this book and have the desire to move from a tumultuous past and to a bountiful future that acknowledges and embraces God's grace and mercy.

Foreword

Apostle Dr. Sonia B. Lee, being crucified with Christ, now lives, yet not she, but Christ that liveth in her; and the life which she now lives in the flesh is lived by faith in the Son of God, who loved her and gave Himself as a ransom for her.

It is both an honor and privilege to have known this great Woman of God as a Friend, Sister and Fellow Laborer in the Body of Christ Jesus. Her life has certainly been a testament of the faithfulness of God, who absolutely does not see us through the lens of men, but through His lens of destiny and purpose. In the eyes of many, she might not have been counted worthy of her calling, but in the divine plans of God, she was called, ordained, and affirmed before being formed in her mother's womb.

Her journey has not been without many dangers, toils, and snares, but through it all, God kept her. Many times, like the shepherd king, when others were ready to turn on her, she had to encourage herself in the Lord with fasting and prayer.

One of the great strengths that I have both observed and admired in this Mighty Woman of God is her bold humility to say, "HELP! I do not know. Teach me." I am delighted and grateful to God to have been able to share, though just a small part, as she navigated through the maze of life's successes and failures, highs and lows, the ups and downs of her spiritual and social journey. She demonstrated great humility when she opted to sit as a student with her ministers in a class God allowed me to offer called "Ministerial Ethics, Etiquette and an Introduction to Homiletics," through Beacon Bible Institute. Not only did she sit, but she unashamedly sought answers to questions pertinent to her growth and development.

Today, I salute Apostle Dr. Sonia B. Lee and the release of her autobiography, which I wholeheartedly endorse, and seek multiplied blessings on you, my sister.

-Bishop Dr. Philip H London

Childhood Dreams

Growing up as a little child in Jamaica, I dreamed of one day becoming a schoolteacher. It ultimately seemed farfetched because of my poor upbringing, but I never let go of that desire completely. I kept believing that one day it would come to pass. Pursuing my education did not provide immediate money or opportunities, so I chose other avenues that I felt, at the time, would keep me going in life for a better future.

Born in the city of Clarendon, I was the second oldest of ten children for my mom and the first child for my dad. My mother's name was Lolie. I do not know where she got her name from, but I guess my grandmother was feeling creative. I've never heard of anybody else named Lolie. A lot of people called her "Hannah," and I'm not sure how that name was derived. Because my mother didn't have the means to support herself and her two young kids at the time, 1 lived with my father, Richard Lee, and his family in May Pen for my early years. I grew up until about age 10 with my dad.

When I moved back with my mother, she was married and

experiencing a lot of hard times financially. She was living in Bunkers Hill, which is in Clarendon, about two hours away from May Pen in what we call "the country." At that time, there was nine of us living in a one-bedroom house. The small dwelling was made of concrete blocks with a rusty zinc roof. We lived in the rural countryside where we could grow our own food, but times were very hard. No matter what we were going through, church was a must for my mother. We had to go every Sunday. I liked to go, and I would lead songs at times. I was a gifted vocalist, so I was somewhat popular in our small community, where most everyone attended church.

We had a large family, but it was wonderful. There was a lot of love and laughs. As the second oldest child, I helped my younger siblings with their daily tasks. I walked with them to school. During times when things were economically hard, I made sure my siblings went to school even when I couldn't go. I tried to push them to have a better education and not to let their current life situation discourage them, as it had me. I wanted them to do and be better, so I was always pushing them to study. There is something about me, as my mother told me from a child coming up, which made me "special." I have a compassionate heart. I always wanted to help, so helping my siblings or helping anyone would never be anything that I would resist because that's just me.

At the same time, it was very rough financially in the family. We would have to go to the market to sell food to make sure we could keep a roof over our heads and to let the other children go to school. My focus was on helping my mother and our family survive at all costs. My dreams would have to wait.

Even when my mother was not feeling well, she still pushed herself to go out and sell fresh produce at the market. I went with her sometimes on the weekends. The conditions were so terrible at times. Sometimes we were working in the hot tropical sun. Sometimes we worked in the pouring rain. We had strong faith that if we maintained a dedicated push, things would eventually work out, though. We always wanted and expected to see a better day, so we did a lot of things to make it. We had a little shop where we sold groceries. We grew some of the food that we were selling, including yams, banana, cabbage, carrots, and peppers. We started at like 7:30 in the morning and worked diligently throughout the day until 5:00. That was the latest we would stay during the week because the kids got home from school at 4:00. After a long day, sometimes I would cook or mom would make dinner.

My father was young and unprepared to take on the full responsibility of taking care of a child. He was a rather care-free young man, in fact. He had eight children, and only two with my mother, who he never married. He was a "road man," someone who stayed out partying and carousing. While my dad never married my mom, he did get married. My mom also got married to my other siblings' father.

My mom was the secretary for the church, and she was well-known and respected. So, when it came to her children, people would always talk. We could never get away with anything negative in public because people in the community would tell her. At 17, I started to get wild and ended up pregnant when I was going to secondary school. No one knew I was pregnant until it was time to have the baby. I hid my pregnancy well because I had a little belly and wore loose clothes. No one suspected anything except for my mother.

I was still going to school every day like normal, but my mother, who is like a seer in the spirit realm, said to me, "Why are you looking so white? You know, it seems as if you're pregnant. Let me check on you."

Because I couldn't ever lie to my mother because she's very spiritual, I said, "Yes, Mom, I'm pregnant. I'm seven months pregnant."

She said, "Oh, my God, you know you can have the baby right now!" She was going crazy about all the things that could go wrong and started questioning me about the baby's father. I reassured her that my baby's father was a good man, and he was until he became unfaithful.

My mom was very supportive. Still, when I got pregnant, she had some shame to come over her because she was a stern mother, and she really lived a God-fearing lifestyle. She couldn't really understand how I came up pregnant. I spent most of my time at school, church or working with her. So, her main thing was how or when did I get pregnant. I got pregnant when I went to spend time with my uncle. I didn't get pregnant in our family home. We all, as children, always made sure to respect our mom, but when we were not around her, we were loose.

I gave birth to my first child, Dorrette, in 1980. Some people talked to me, but they never supported me. I knew better than getting pregnant, but the damage was done. They always say the first one was a mistake, which can be forgiven, but the second one was not a mistake. It's a choice.

Two years after having my daughter, I gave birth to another daughter in 1982. I named her Natalee. My mother was a patient woman. She supported her children unconditionally, but she gave us some hard teachings too. She was certainly not glad about me being pregnant again, but she would never turn me away. I could always go home if I really needed. When I came up pregnant for the second time, she said to me, "Oh, come on now, Sonia. I think more or less that you would further your education." She would literally beg me to finish school.

I'm sure she would have preferred that I was married at the very least before having children. In my mind, marriage was not for me because of what I witnessed in my mom's marriage. From a child, I witnessed seeing my mother's marriage not being good. My mother told me that I would get married one day. However, I have always said that I don't want to get married because I don't want to get divorced. At church, the pastor always told us about not getting divorced because God "hates divorce" (Malachi 2:16, NKJV). I was taught that and other teachings about women staying committed to their families no matter what, and that influenced me as I grew up. I said to myself, *"Man, I don't want to get married and divorced."* I have never been married until this day for fear of being mistreated and then being trapped. I really can't put up with unfaithfulness or abuse of any kind from a man because I know how I should be treated. Despite what I have been through with men, I never lost my self-esteem. I know how I am supposed to be treated, and once I'm not getting that, I'm out of the relationship.

After getting pregnant with the second child, I moved out my mom's house and I went to live with my uncle. To my surprise, when I got pregnant again, my mother said to me, "Come, my daughter. Come home."

I didn't want to go back home, though. I wanted to avoid the shame and questions. Because my mother had always been very helpful in our church, a lot of people looked up to her. So, I just really wanted to stay away with this pregnancy. However, she said, "No, no, no, no, no. Come home to mama. This is my grandchild. I don't like what you did, but I'm not going to turn my back on you." My mother got pregnant when she was 18 years old, and my grandmother helped her, and that inspired her to help me. She added, "I didn't see my mother turn me away or anything like that. It's dangerous for you. You don't know what's going to happen. If you get sick, you may need help with the baby. So, I want you to be here." So, I went back home.

People did talk about me and probably looked down on our family. At one point, there was a little issue in the church about it, but we overcame it. People talk bad about you for having a daughter in the house pregnant who is not married. I was hurt, not for myself, though, for my mother. I felt I needed to go say something to the people at the church to defend her honor. My mother was like this, however. She always said, "I don't need you to talk for me. I can talk for myself."

She went to church, and she told them, "My daughter didn't get pregnant in my house, but I told her to come home." Once she said that, the matter was settled.

CHAPTER 2

Turning Point

My mother used to say this phrase to me: "Show me your company, and I will tell you who you are." I got caught up with the wrong company, dropped out of school and had my first child. I think that was the beginning of a whirlwind of events to impact my life negatively. However, something triggered that behavior. Something stole my innocence, turning hurt into turmoil.

One afternoon after leaving a school graduation, I was walking home with a large group of people. One of the most notorious men in the community was walking towards me. He wasn't coming up to me like he wanted to hurt me; he approached me like he wanted to talk. He strolled into the crowd of youth and pulled me out with all those other children walking alongside me. He was a tall, muscular, handsome man known for having his way with women. He was clean cut and friendly to most people, so when this happened, it wasn't alarming. No one even said anything to him, as if it was a normal occurrence. When he initially approached me, I ignored him, so I believe he was angry I wouldn't talk to him.

He may have probably still done it if I would have spoken to him. He was used to getting what he wanted.

After abducting me, he took me to a house in a densely wooded area. He forcibly ushered me into the cellar. Terrified and still shocked by his brazen actions, I didn't fight back. My focus was on surviving and escaping. He sexually assaulted me in the cellar, where no one could see or hear anything. Then he took me back outside, deeper into the woods. I then heard him calling out three different men's names to come join in as well. The plan was for them to have intercourse with me too. When he called them, I listened to every word of the conversation. He told them that he had locked the door, and I was not going to be able to get out. When he told them how to pull the door to get to me, I listened intently. So, while he was on the phone telling them what to do, I started to look around to see what I could use to get out of the house and how I would go about it. Eventually, he left and told them that he would be back shortly. Apparently, they were not far away. I checked the door and it was not difficult to open. I took off running, not sure where I was or which direction to go. I was trying to get as far away from there as possible. I was a track star at school, a 100-meter runner who was rarely defeated. It was around one o'clock in the day, so I had enough light to see where I was going. I kept running in that forest, and I ran for about three miles straight until I got near to a school. When I heard some people talking in the distance, I said to myself, "*I'm almost there.*"

When I ran out of the bush, I ran directly into the roadway. However, I didn't worry about any cars by this point. I was worried about being taken again, and I needed to be seen publicly. When I almost got to the end of the road, I heard someone say, "That sounds like Sonia. That sounds like Sonia's voice." I was crying for help and sobbing. Because I used to sing at church, a lot of people knew my voice. They knew my mom and my family.

To my joy, a man saw me and said, "That's Sonia"

I said, "Yes, it's me!" I then broke down and started to cry uncontrollably, pleading my case to this man. "Why me?" I questioned. "Is that fair?"

He seemed as if he knew what happened before I started to tell him. It seemed that everyone knew, but no one was prepared to do anything about it. The guy, my offender, was a former soldier who even the local police were afraid of confronting. He was never convicted or even arrested, and until this day, I don't know whatever happened to that guy.

After that, I stopped trusting men and began to self-destruct. Once I started to date after that, I became pregnant a year later. In those days, having a baby at a young age was a disappointment to your parents, who knew the perils of unwed motherhood at a young age, especially in poor families. Their desire was to see their kids excel beyond them, and a child would hold you back. I can't totally blame the assault on my pregnancy, but I was broken. As a defense mechanism, I became hard and intolerant of any abusive behavior.

If I was in a relationship and the man was aggressive or talked to me hard in any shape or form, I was gone. I never trusted men for the most part. If I saw any red flags, I was done. I saw how my mother was treated, and I wanted better than that. The biblical story of the prophet Hosea and his unfaithful wife, Gomer, is a great inspiration of obedience and God's mercy. Hosea took his wife back after she went off into prostitution, literally buying her back just so God could get a testimony out of him for the disobedient Israelites. I said to myself, "*You know what? Let me tell you, God, I couldn't deal with something like that even for your sake.*" God allows bad things to happen to us sometimes for our or His greater good, but I wanted no parts of unfaithfulness in my life. I decided I would either fight (verbally or physically) or simply leave bad situations. At that time, I was not spiritually mature enough to allow God to use me for a testimony. Later on in life, I would find out that sometimes we have no choice.

By this time, I was struggling to raise two children and life didn't seem like it was getting any better. During this time, I had another tragic turning point, but the battle was not financial or emotional, things I had gotten used to fighting. It became medical.

I was diagnosed with breast cancer at the age of 23. I found a lump in my breast after my second daughter, Natalee, was born. I went to the doctor, and they performed several tests and said I must come back for surgery. So, I told my mother what the doctor's office advised, and she said, "If you have cancer, you have to get the cancer out."

I replied, "Mama, I see God do things for you all the time, so why don't you think that God can't heal me and I don't have to get any surgery?"

Mama said, "Well, my daughter, I cannot say anything because faith is what your mother has lived by, and you're going to exercise it. I can't say anything about that."

The doctor scheduled me for surgery to remove the lump. A week before the surgery, I went to bed and got one of the strangest dreams in my life. I dreamed that a strange man talked to me, but the man looked just like Natalee's father. He came to me and said, "Your sickness is not unto death. I want you to go and get this, and scrape it and drink it." He held up an aloe plant. In Jamaica, we call it "sinkle bible." He told me to drink it for seven mornings. He continued, "When you go back to the doctor, the doctor will not see any cancer."

In the dream, I tried to respond to him and ask questions. I said to him, "Hold on. Hold on. Hold on. Please, please, please, please, please, let me talk to you. Let me talk to you." And until this day, I've never seen him in real life or in a dream again. The man literally vanished, and I didn't get to hear or say anything more.

I told my mother and father about the dream, and my mother directed me to follow through on the instructions to drink aloe each day. I did exactly as instructed for the next week. When I went back to the doctor for surgery, he asked me how I had been feeling and performed another medical exam. He said, "There's no cancer." They showed me all my lab results, and everything was normal.

The nurse said, "Sonia, you have no cancer!" They were just as shocked as me.

I have no cancer until today. I have shared my testimony of healing with others, and one lady asked me how I'm still alive. "You sound like a dead person," she said. "All these things you are telling me can't be possible."

"Yes," I assured her, "they are."

Throughout the years, I have gone back to get medical checkups, but nothing like that has ever been diagnosed or even suspected.

CHAPTER 3

Dealing with Motherhood

In my mother's marriage, I saw her husband was unfaithful to her, and it grew this resentment in my heart. All of us as sisters, we have this thing about us that we don't want to go through what our mother had been through. Until she died, she never divorced or remarried, so she stayed in the marriage knowing that he was cheating. At one point, he moved out and basically abandoned her. When he left, the family's financial struggle really began. That's when I decided that I would have to travel to seek a better life so I can help my mother. My brothers and sisters were doing well in school, so I felt they would be okay. Eventually, three of them became teachers, and I was so proud.

My dad migrated to the United States, where he decided to reside permanently, and my close relationship with him really motivated me to be where he was. So, I got my visa and started to travel back and forth to the U.S., where he was looking toward fulfilling his own dream and embracing "the land of opportunity." There are so many things that you can achieve in life if you just stay focused. I believe that it's not always the path that you desire that's going to take you to your destination, but you'll get there if you just keep going. I realize in life that your dream can detour down many different paths, but it's never over until you decide it's over. That is the mindset that kept me going on my journey to greater success.

After traveling back and forth from Jamaica to the U.S., I started buying and selling different merchandise for many years. When the opportunity to travel abroad and work presented itself, I immediately jumped at the chance. I started traveling to various islands in the Caribbean, trying to make life better for me and my children. Giving up was not an option because if I didn't work, then we wouldn't eat, as the Bible notes in 2 Thessalonians 3:10. Leaving my children was one of the hardest decisions that I ever had to make in my life, but life doesn't always present itself clearly at the starting point. Things were rough. Lessons came hard. Grace and mercy was all I had.

I moved to the Cayman Islands when Natalee was 7 years old. However, before I left Jamaica, I got involved with this guy and thought things would work out, but they didn't. Afterward, I left for Cayman Islands. When I got there, I discovered that I was pregnant again. I went back to Jamaica to give birth. My family was surprised at both my return and pregnancy. I was happy to be reunited with my mother and daughters, but I knew I would only be staying for a little while. I had to finish my journey to carve out a better life, anywhere but Jamaica. After giving birth to my first and only son, Shae, I started thinking about my next move abroad and what I would do for work.

I was a very hands-on mother when I was with my children. Thus, when I went abroad for work, it was tough leaving every time. I just didn't want to drag them through my upheaval and instability until I got to where I needed to be. My children really had great fathers except for one. In fact, if it hadn't been for their fathers, I might not have even been able to travel for work. Motherhood and working abroad was challenging. I wanted to be there more, but I was essentially just running and looking for opportunities, always thinking I was making the best decisions for myself and my children. Throughout my life, I had to make a lot of sacrifices and tough decisions regarding family and work. Still, if those circumstances would bring me to where I am today, except for a couple of adjustments, I wouldn't have had it any other way.

I always thought that I could choose the way I wanted to live and do whatever I wanted to do, but that didn't work out as I expected. Proverbs 14:12 says: "There's a way which seemeth right to a man, but the end thereof are the ways of death." Nothing that I tried seemed to satisfy my mind or heart. I just kept failing and feeling empty, going to nightclubs from Thursday night through Sunday morning. I was trying to fill the emptiness in my life. Before it was the clubs, it was me dropping out of school and trying to get into relationships that seemed productive. After being sexually assaulted, it would be many years or decades before I got my healing. I was *trying* to be a woman instead of embracing what was already mine. I was looking for love in all the wrong places and from all the wrong people. Some may call me "promiscuous" or "loose." However, the best word to describe me at the time was "lost." My love tank was empty, and I was running around trying to fill that void with external things and people. I needed to learn to love, accept and value myself. More importantly, I needed to know that God is love and His grace is sufficient. I didn't need to do or be anything more because He loved me as is, broken and all. During that time in my life, it was only God's grace and heavenly mercies that kept me.

The word of God was instilled in me growing up in Sunday school, including scriptures like Proverbs 3:6, which says, "In all your ways acknowledge Him, and He shall direct your path." So, when we don't allow God to have His way in our lives, we will always experience roadblocks. I, nevertheless, strayed after learning the Word and knowing Him, and I faced my grave obstacles as a result.

I don't see the many challenges that I went through in life as failures; instead, I regard them as steppingstones toward my future. I've learned that whatever I go through may not just be for me, but it may be a situation that helps or even inspires others. I would later learn that. Meanwhile, I was still learning lessons my mother had been trying to teach me.

Being sexually assaulted at a young age was a big factor in me not being able to trust others, but I never let that distrust stop me from pursuing my dreams. Still, being hurt will definitely change you. As a child growing up, I always wanted to be a teacher, and I tried hard to get there. However, I did not continue in the direction that would take me there once I started having children. Instead of me teaching others, life was about to start teaching me some valuable lessons.

CHAPTER 4

Living Abroad

There are times in life when we have to make tough choices that will affect or impact those we love. The devil, who is a thief, comes to steal, kill and destroy, but Christ came to give life more abundantly (John 10:10). As a mother, I had tough choices to make that I felt would provide a more abundant life for my children. Traveling to other countries for work was what I convinced myself was best for me and the best way to support my children.

After moving to Antigua in 1985, I worked at a high-end French and Italian restaurant as a chef for the first time. I had never been trained or worked as a cook of any kind before. I learned fast and worked my way up in the restaurant, and no one trained me. I initially went there to wash dishes and clean the tables, but in about three months, I became a cook. While I was washing dishes and during my breaks, I would watch the main chef prepare the meals and use culinary techniques. I worked as a chef there for seven years. I was a great chef if I must say so myself. I also worked as a housekeeper and did other types of domestic jobs while living in Antigua.

I went to Antigua with a cousin of mine. It was a lot of confusion when we arrived. We had an issue with immigration and no means of transportation. I didn't know this until I arrived because she told me that her cousin was coming to get us. When we went outside, she started talking to this unidentified man. I wasn't paying much attention to what they were saying. All I know, a couple minutes later, she was signaling me to come over to where her and the guy was talking. She said, "Come on, let's go. We are getting a ride."

I went along with her. When we get to the hotel, it was all police and law enforcement everywhere. They were looking for the man who had given us a ride. The next day, it's all we heard about. God was by my side even before I got to know him. I had a praying mother, and I know her prayers kept me. The next day, we were supposed to leave the island, but while we were walking, this car came up and a man asked if we needed a ride. He says, "It seems as if you ladies are tired."

I said without hesitation, "Well of course we are!"

"My office is just right around the way," he said. He stopped to get us water. We came to find out that he was the secretary of the Prime Minister. I told him that the authorities said we could only spend one day in the country. He then took our passports and got some more time for us in that country.

While living in Antigua, I got pregnant with my fourth child, Ann Marie. My three children were back in Jamaica with my mother and their fathers. Natalee was with her father, and Dorrette and Shae was with my mother. Ann Marie was born in Antigua in November 1990, and I was doing better financially. I had my own apartment at this time. My child's father made sure I was taken care of. He supported me through my whole pregnancy. He was there for anything I needed.

Anne Marie's father was an older man who I honestly thought would do better by me, and on the surface, he was wonderful. I later found out that he was also involved with someone else. You know, they always say, "When you are in sin, you just sin." What it was all really about was me trying to get to where I wanted to be in life, but I was going about it all wrong – without God. I didn't know how to stop myself and correct my life's course. All I knew how to do was keep going, but what I didn't realize was that I was actually going backwards, not forward. I suffered a lot of heartbreak, and having children while trying to get my life together made it even more challenging. Every time I had a baby, it slowed me down. I would never give up, though.

I had been communicating with my father in the United States, and I decided my next attempt at "getting it together" would be there. Ann Marie remained in Antigua with her father, and I moved to South Florida, where my father was living with his wife, Bernice. I had lived in Antigua for many years, so leaving my child temporarily and everything else behind was hard. I felt like a new place would provide a fresh start and new opportunities. What I didn't know was that if the heart and mind were not transformed, the circumstances would be the same, no matter where you move.

CHAPTER 5

Coming to the Land of Opportunity

Nursing was not a part of my dream but it was the path that I took as it presented itself. I did that for many years until it became a passion to take care of the elderly. The money was good but not my main reason to show up every day. Family is important to me and many of my patients did not have a close relationship with their own family, so we developed a close bond together. That it how I survived in America on a work visa.

While living and working in America, I got pregnant for the fifth and final time with my daughter Kerlande. I had her in America with a Haitian-American army veteran who liked to party with me at local clubs. Kerlande's dad was terrible. While I was in the hospital giving birth in July 1995, he came in with another woman pregnant for him. When I left the hospital, I said he would never look me in the face again. So, I struggled as a single parent with Kerlande. I heard that he died when she was about 12 years old. Apparently, he went back to the army. When I met him, he had just gotten out of the army. After re-enlisting, a woman stabbed him to death.

I stayed in contact with my dad when I got here. He told

me having another baby, Kerlande, would slow me down. It was my baby, and my mind was made up. I wasn't living with him at that time, but he said, "I think you should put off having another baby and see if you could better your life." He gave me a good talk as a dad, but there was nothing that he could do or say to change my mind. Anne Marie was still in Antigua with her father at the time, but I later got her here with me. Dorrette's father got her here. Natalee and Shae were in Jamaica with my mother, but later they joined me here in the United States. Kerlande was born here. All of my children eventually got to the United States with me, but it wasn't easy.

My life went downhill again because I was merely working to pay babysitters. A friend saw me struggling and she offered to keep the baby for me until I got on my feet. So, that's when I was able to work full-time and save some money for the first time. I left Kerlande with my friend during the week and went to work a live-in-job as a home health aide. I would come home on the weekends. I missed my children, but I knew we needed the money to get our own place. I worked for like five months straight and saved all of that money and got myself an apartment. At this point, I could afford for some-one to come and stay with her. Once Anne Marie came to live with me, I got another job that I could come home every afternoon. Meanwhile, I partied a lot while in the U.S. like I had throughout much of my young adult life. I went to the club every night starting Thursday through Sunday. I would come home Monday morning like 1or 2 a.m. I loved dancing and carousing with people who I thought could make me happy. I would have to pay a babysitter to watch Anne Marie and Kerlande on those nights.

It was in America that the course of my life would change forever, though. God began to call me. Before, He would always let me know He is there, but when I got to America, it was more than a call. It was a calling, a call home where I would form a new family and priorities. We cannot serve two masters: the world and God. I've learned that anything that has two heads is a monster. God was trying to show me enjoyment, or better yet fulfillment, through another means.

Nobody talks about God quite like me. I grew up in church and I saw all the blessings that God has given to my mother. So, I knew that there was a real God, but I was never ready to serve Him. Serving God would prevent me from doing certain things that I wanted to do.

One night, while I was getting my hair ready and my clothes were lying on the bed to go out partying, I decided that I was ready to surrender my will to the Lord. My girlfriend called and said, "I didn't hear from you. What happened? You're not going to the club tonight."

I replied, "I don't feel well."

She said, "What do you mean? I spoke to you like an hour ago. What happened?"

I told her that "the Lord is calling me" just plain as that.

"You sound like you're crazy!"

I explained, "I'm not crazy. I believe that the Lord is calling me."

She said, "I've never heard anything like this in my life."

At this point, I got rough with her. Growing up, I was the sibling that was always ready to fight. I didn't take or put up with anyone's foolishness or threats. My friend offended me, and I was getting upset because I was trying to explain to her how I was feeling differently. "I'm being called for a greater purpose," I said.

She said, "What do you mean?"

I said, "God is calling me. I really think my time is up."

She said, "You know what, let me get off the phone with you."

I was seeing this guy, and he came by my place. I was suddenly turned off by him for some reason. I didn't want him to touch me. When he reached for me, I said, "Don't touch me." He asked if there was something wrong with me. I said, "Yes, something is wrong with me. God is calling me." By now, both he and my friend had called me "crazy." So I told him, "I'm crazy enough to put you out of my place." He went away and I never saw him again.

After three days, I had another friend who called me and said she was going to host prayer meeting at her house and wanted to see if I wanted to attend. I said sure. When I went to the prayer meeting, there was a female pastor there. She was preaching so passionately about God calling you to do his work. She wasn't looking directly at me or anything. She was just preaching. However, I somehow knew that God gave her that message for me. While I sat down there, I felt my foot starting to shake, and I thought, "What on earth is going on? I cannot stop my feet." I couldn't figure out what was going on with me. I began to question myself, saying, "What is wrong with me? I can't control my body." Well, I didn't know what was happening, and when I did realize my situation, I was on the floor. I fell on my face. The Lord was having His way with me. Meanwhile, the pastor said, "Are you willing to surrender?"

I said, "Yes."

After that encounter, I started going to that pastor's church on Sunday. After being there for six months, she asked me if I want to get baptized. And

I said to her, "I'm not ready."

She was relentless and coming at me extremely hard. To that, I explained, "I don't think you should be forcing me to get baptized. I think that is something I should do on my own will." There was something the pastor didn't know, though. I didn't want to get baptized because I had a sister named Claudia living in South Florida, and I hadn't spoken to her for over a year. Growing up in church, I learned that you cannot have unforgiveness in your heart. Given that understanding, I decided that I would not get baptized until I made it right with my sister.

One Friday while I was in prayer, the Lord brought up my sister in front of my face. I said, "Okay." I was taking the bus to work that day, and when I went to the bus station in the morning, I saw my sister Claudia. I said, "Claudia, how are you?"

Trying to avoid me, she looked away because she was stuck. She asked, "You're talking to me?"

Sarcastically, I asked, "That's your name, right?"

She said, "Yes, that's my name, but I didn't expect you to come and call me like that you know. You're calling me like we were talking all this time."

I explained, "Well, I've changed my life. I decided to serve the Lord, and I know that I have to make things right."

She started crying, and she hugged me. We made it right that day. So, the next Sunday, I told my leader that I wanted to get baptized, and so I got baptized that very Sunday. From that point, I became a dedicated steward in church, trying to help and make myself useful in any way possible. I would sweep floors at the church. I took on the rough part in the ministry. I cleaned every inch of that building, and I did so for seven years, very faithfully, until I got ordained as an evangelist. Later on, I got ordained as a pastor in training. I stayed in that church for a while and then went to another one before God would put me on my own path.

As I sought God, others in my life became more distant, feeling as if I had no time for them. I spent every free moment I could seeking God and serving in the ministry in any way I could. I kept running to church because I sincerely wanted to know God. Because I had been so wretched, I wanted

Him to cleanse my heart and renew my mind, giving me new priorities. During the week, I was at Bible study or prayer meeting. On the weekends, I was at service throughout the day. On holidays, I wanted to ensure I honored God by serving the community. Some members of my family thought that I didn't want to have a relationship with them because of my allegiance to the church. That wasn't the case, though. I just wanted to know more about the Lord. The Bible in James 4:8, says, "Draw near to God, and he will draw near to you." Having a wedge in my family wasn't the only challenge I would face in surrendering completely to God.

After accepting the office of the Apostle, then came another wave of trials. I fell and broke my ankle and was in a wheelchair for eight months. My stepmother, Bernice, took sick following my mother, and they both went into a coma, one behind another. They ultimately died in the very same order in which they got sick. Those were some trials that almost crippled my mind. But God is always faithful, for He kept my mind. He gave me strength and endurance through it all. I've never been through so much change in my life after I gave my heart to the Lord. It was a new chapter to build my faith, and it was certainly painful. I got evicted every three to six months. I was losing jobs and I had two children depending on me, watching my every move. Things were falling apart, but when God is involved, things fall apart to come together better (Romans 8:28). Everything was a mess. I had broken my leg, and the doctor said if I didn't have surgery, I would never walk again. I went one year and eight months without running water in my house, having to carry water from outside to bathe me and my children. If that wasn't bad enough, one of my daughters got into a terrible car accident. While she was in the hospital, the next day, a truck ran off the road and into my bedroom while I was asleep. It missed striking me directly within inches.

It's like I had money. My bills were paid, but I had no peace. I wasn't sick, but my head was exploding. It was a funny feeling. Many times in life, we feel as though money can give us happiness and the joy that we so desire. However, I know from experience that until we choose the right path, we will never have the peace that God promised us. I had lots of people around me at parties and in nightclubs, but I was still lonely. It was such a funny feeling. Eventually, when I accepted the call to Christ, all I could say to everybody was that "the Lord is calling me." That is what came out of my mouth every time someone asked me what was wrong. "The Lord is calling me, and I don't want to be around a man. I don't want to be around woman. I'm not going to the party. That's it for me." It was time for change, a major one. I knew I had a praying mother. To be honest, out of all her children, I was the bad one. I'm the one she worried about the most. So, I know that it was God just pulling me out of worldly things that I was really focused on and that would cost me my soul if I didn't change.

My current circle of friends and acquaintances started to turn against me when I gave my heart to the Lord. I was running away from them to Him with everything I had left. I wanted to know more about God, to be closer to Him. I made up my mind to be strict in my walk with God. When I talked to people about all the things that God has brought me through, I wanted people to understand why I was sold out to Him. I always told my mother that "when I get saved, I'm going to stay saved. I'm one of your children that is going to stay saved." When I first got saved, I was so zealous and sold out for God it became a conflict in the family. I was always going to church and I seemed to pull away from everyone. When I started to run like that for God and not the world, now everybody, including my mother, father and children, just seemed to turn against me. They would get so annoyed because I was always running to the church, missing outings and family functions. What they all didn't know was how much I was going through, and church provided comfort and hope. At times, I was avoiding my family, particularly my mother, because I didn't want her to know everything I was going through. She was one who liked to worry, and I surely didn't want to cause her anymore stress or be responsible for her getting a stress-related illness like high blood pressure or heart problems. Only one of my children, Natalee, decided that her mother was not being extreme or too excessive. She told them, "Mommy is not that type of person. I think mommy just needs some time." I clearly remember her saying that because it brought me some comfort. I felt like I was forsaken by most everyone I loved. Even to this day, of one my children doesn't really desire to have a relationship with me.

During this time, I was staying with Dorrette's father's family when I got the calling to pastor. I was running from the calling, though. Eventually, I started the ministry in the lady's house where we were staying. We started out doing a prayer service, but we eventually had to move to a building. I started in an office space for $300 per month with my two youngest children and one member. Sixteen years later, we are still going strong. I thanked God for his protection and provision that kept me. Every elevation comes with new trials to deal with, so in other words, the higher the level, the greater the challenges that you have to overcome. It wasn't an easy task, but I had to get to a place where I said, "Lord, I cannot trace you, but I will trust you."

I think I spoke too soon because shortly thereafter came another episode where I had to continue to trust God. In 2014, I received my United States Citizenship and decided to take a trip to London, England, to visit my siblings, When I got there, I keep feeling that something was about to happen. I spent two weeks there and came back with the same feeling. I went to church that Tuesday night and told the members that we have to pray because I didn't like what I was feeling. That afternoon, I called my daughter Ann Marie and told her that she should be careful driving because I saw a vision of her car turning over in an accident. Twenty minutes after that, she crashed, and her car was totaled. She only came out with a few scratches, though. That was on Monday.

During the night on Tuesday, November 18, 2014, she went to the hospital with my youngest daughter, Kerlande, who was pregnant. When Kerlande came home, she wanted to sleep in my bedroom. I told her no, but she insisted. I opened my bedroom door and directed her to her own room. Shortly thereafter, I went to bed. At 5:10 a.m., a neighbor's pickup truck drove through my bedroom and knocked over the sofa my daughter wanted to sleep on that night in my room. I think the driver was going to dump leaves and branches from yard cuttings. The bricks from the wall and debris from the truck were all over my bed. Branches were everywhere. The impact from the truck caused a couch in the living room to somehow fly across the room, almost hitting me. The truck struck me while in bed, and I landed on my dresser on the other side. The truck stopped after striking my bed. All the blocks from the wall fell on me, but God brought me out safely. Ann Marie, who was still wearing her hospital gown from the day before was startled but grateful that I was okay. She and Kerlande rushed to get me out the house to safety.

I was surprised and so was my neighbor, Jean Prosper, because he said that his truck's brakes suddenly failed. Apparently, he was backing out his driveway at the house directly in front of mine. He was mashing the truck's brake pedal to make it stop, but "nothing" happened. He said, "I felt someone took a hold of the steering wheel because I was no longer in control." He was puzzled as to how he missed the car parked outside my house and ended up instead driving into my house.

The television news crew came to the scene as well, and they were asking where is the body of the person who died in the crash because they couldn't believe that anyone could survive a terrible accident like that. I yelled, "It's me! I'm not dead. I'm right here." They all looked at me in astonishment. The devil was so mad and wanted to take me out, but he cannot kill who God wants to live. Still, it took months before I started to have a clear mind.

I felt like Job when I first came to America. It took years to rebuild my foundation, but God saw me through it. The Bible says in the book of Job 13:15, "Though He slay me, yet will I trust in Him: but I will maintain mine own ways before him." There was a time when I felt as if I just couldn't get a break from problems, but there are some sinful ways in our life that require a greater pressure of trials to correct. For instance, the spirit of pride doesn't allow us to see ourselves as we truly are, so we project a sense of perfection. God has to break that in order for us to serve Him or others. God allows trials in our lives to develop good character, and while it didn't always feel good, the goal is for us to be better citizens in the kingdom of God. Today, I can say I am better, not bitter.

CHAPTER 6

The Unexpected Process

After accepting the Lord, my life began to change daily but not for the good. Having five children as a single mother in a new country without family support, I went through lots of financial, personal and domestic hardships. This included living with other people, sometimes sleeping on the floor and chairs, and not being treated well by those who were supposed to be helping me. I never gave up on God, though. We cannot embrace difficult times without the Holy Spirit. Amongst other things, the Holy Spirit is a teacher, providing wisdom and insight. So, the infilling of the Holy Spirit is the beginning of a life of upgrade. It teaches us all truth. The Bible says in John 4:24 that "God is a spirit and they that worship Him must worship Him in spirit and in truth." Knowing His promises and who He is was all that kept me sane and hopeful at times.

When I gave my heart to the Lord, I expected things to turnaround overnight. Growing up, I always thought that when people accept the Lord, everything is going to be okay in their lives. What I didn't realize is that when you come to the Lord, there is a slow transformation process that you have to experience. Much of it relates to Him wanting to build our character and strength so that we are not just getting blessings, but we become a blessing to others. When I started to see major challenges and bad situations happening after I got saved, I would wonder and question why all those things were happening now. I was unable to keep a job for long, so my financial situation and home life was in turmoil. In going back and forth with the job situation, things got rough and we ended up losing our place several times. My youngest kids (Ann Marie and Kerlande) and I had to live with different family members and friends at times. My daughter Natalee got married and was living with her husband, Andre. I had a standard job like three to five months before it was back to square one: finding a job and new place to live. The only thing I never lost was my faith in God. I continue to remain steadfast, knowing He would never leave or forsake me. I keep focused on His word and promises. Through it all, I stayed with Him, never going back to my former ways. I believe the Scripture when it says "the battle is not yours, it belongs to the Lord" (2 Chronicles 20:15). The Bible also says that God is our refuge and strength, and a very present help in the time of trouble (Psalm 46). And so each time that I faced tough times, people would ask me what I did in my life so bad to be going through so much. It was so bad that I felt that I could relate to Job's trials because we were living here and there without consistent income. It was a disaster.

We went through a lot of evictions during this time. We suffered 18 evictions in total. The instability and shame of the evictions were very hard on my children. I do believe the hardest thing with the moving around to different schools was them having to start over with friends. They would start at a school and get to meet new friends there. Then they would have to leave those friends over there to make new friends over here where we were now living. So, all the moving was very hard for them emotionally and socially.

After having experienced 17 evictions and now facing my 18th, I went on the balcony of the apartment to talk to God. I had to go to court to face a judge in the morning concerning my eviction, so I was worried. As I stood out there facing the heavens, I said, "Lord, you got to talk to me. I don't even know what to put on this paper." I had a couple of options: just move out; pay up all the money owed and stay; or make an appeal of some kind to the court. I had chosen the last option, but I didn't know exactly what to say. I just knew my answer needed to describe my circumstances and provide reasons that may help stop the eviction. My court date was the next morning, and I was nervous but determined to draft something in writing. In case I got to court late, I could leave my written appeal with the clerk, and it could still be taken to the judge for consideration.

When the Lord had me to start writing, I ended up writing around three full pages front and back. I took it to the courthouse in the morning. By the time I arrived, there was another challenge because I got there late just as I had feared. The court clerk told me that I could not see the judge. It was too late. She said she couldn't take that letter to the judge because I was not going to get the kind of help I was seeking. "All you need to do is to pay the money owed," she said.

"I don't think you should make that decision here," I said. "Why not take the letter to the judge?"

With that, she said she would take it up to the judge. "Okay," she said, "you can go ahead. You will hear back from us."

I left the courthouse not knowing what would happen. *Would the clerk even give the judge my letter?* It was out of my control, but I knew I had done as the Spirit led me. Eventually, when I did hear back from the court, the letter stated that I was being given three more months in the apartment. God is such a miracle worker! God extended my time, giving me an opportunity to stay in the apartment while I found work.

After three months, I still didn't have a job, so I got evicted after that. They wouldn't give me any more chances. After that eviction, it is so ironic, things settled down. I was finally able to find and maintain consistent living arrangements. I found a nice duplex after all those evictions. Prior to this, the Lord had said to me, "Who is your judge and your lawyer?" I cried out and responded, "You, Lord," and he showed up for me. He started making provisions that only His miraculous hand could provide. It was like the best thing I ever experienced. Once I was settled down into my own place with the Lord's help, who provided so much for me, I thought that was the end of my problems.

By this time, all of my siblings and my mother got their visa to come to the United States. Before their arrival, I went to the store to get the merchandise that I had placed on layaway for my family. As I went to pick up everything, I was saying to myself, "*I'm getting everything ready for them early.*" Then when I went to get food for the church because we feed the less fortunate in the community, I fell and broke my ankle. This happened one week before everyone came to town. By the time my mother and all my siblings arrived, I was in a wheelchair. I wasn't even able to pick them up from the airport. I was so disappointed. I had to make all kinds of arrangements to get them. Despite my discouragement about my physical state and inability to drive my family around, I realized that I had to be grateful to be alive. I had fallen on the back of my head, but God turned it around so only my ankle was broken, not my skull.

I planned a celebration for my family, friends and members of the church at a hotel in Coral Springs. It was somewhat of a family reunion with my family coming from abroad, including my mother. I have a lot of church family, and so everybody came to know my family personally. So, it was not only my own family and friends, but also members of the church who attended the celebration. It was a huge get-together. I was so excited to show my mother and siblings how much better I was doing and how I had finally gotten a church family.

After the celebration and everyone went back home, I sent my mother barrels with all kinds of necessary home goods, food and just about everything I thought she needed or wanted. My mom was so excited. She called me and said, "Sonia, you know I love to give, but I just felt in my heart that I must be led by God to give. The last time you sent things for me, I just gave it all away, and then I end up in need."

I said, "Well, Mama, that's what you taught us, how to give to others. You taught us to give but just give in moderation, how to give and keep some for yourself."

When my mother went back to Jamaica, she would call me like three times a week. We had such a great bond after she came to visit. I didn't get my immigration papers or green card until about 14 years after being in the United States. That meant I couldn't officially settle in the U.S. or anything like that. After I got it, I just went home to Jamaica one time. So, it had been a long time since I had seen her. One day, she called me, and she said she was not feeling well. She told me she went to the doctor. She didn't have any diabetes or high blood pressure. I said, "To God be the glory."

"At my age, everything is okay," but she said, "I don't understand because I'm still not feeling well." She was 79 years old at this time. One of my sisters decided to let her go to Kingston to see a better doctor. When she went there, the doctor sent her to the hospital. She was at the hospital for about four days. After four days, she went into a coma. Then after she went into a coma, the following week, my stepmother, my father's wife, took sick and ended up in the hospital. So, the Wednesday, my mother went into coma, and the next Wednesday, my stepmother went into coma. The following week after that, my mother died, and the next week, my stepmother died. They took sick a week apart, and they died a week apart. It wasn't easy for my family in any sense. It was like a sudden shock to them because she just took sick and died. There were no warning signs or anything that would prepare us for the loss. She didn't spend a long time suffering or in the hospital. So, it was shocking. I mean, it was so shocking.

I had a sinking feeling before she passed. Given this sense, I went to bed and decided that I was going to turn off my phone because I felt as if I was not going to get good news in the morning. I turned my phone off completely, not just the ringer, after hearing everything the doctor said and what my brothers and sisters said about her condition. In the morning, I got up and was taking Natalee to work when I turned my phone back on. I saw that my sister had been calling me. When I called her back, she asked if I heard from my brother in England. I told her I hadn't. She said they had all been calling me from morning. I said, "I know they've been calling because mama died." And she said yes.

She said, "Sis, why did you just take it like that?"

I said, "I don't know."

When I was going to my bed, I just had this feeling I couldn't shake. So that's why I carried my phone to bed and turned it off. I didn't want them to call during the night to tell me the bad news. Eventually, they said she died at 4:30 before day in the morning. All I know is that she went to a place of rest because the Bible says to be absent from the body is to be present with the Lord (2 Corinthians 5:8).

We always experience loses of some kind, and in order to go on and not give up on tomorrow, we must know we can recover from them. Grieving is a process that we often undergo after significant loses. We can get lost or stuck in grief if we are not careful. It's only when we believe the word of God, trusting that He can comfort and keep us in all things as He promised (Deut. 31:8; Joshua 1:9, Matt. 5:4; John 16:22), that we can overcome in our life. Losing my mother felt like it was too much to take. I know we have to work out our faith, but all the hardships almost seemed too challenging for me. Still, I kept the faith.

CHAPTER 7

Finding the Father

Moving forward in life, I came upon many dream-killers who had their point of view of how my life would turn out, but I have learned that listening to other people's opinions and suggestions do not always add value to your life. For instance, taking advice from someone who did not make it in the same area of life that you are trying to pursue, can be a hindrance in your pathway. My life was definitely a roller coaster, but when I think things over, I'm happy it all worked out for the ultimate outcome of getting to know the Heavenly Father.

The best decision I've made in my life is to serve the Lord and fall in love with Him. Romans 8:28 says, "And we know that all things work together for good to them that love God, to them who are the called according to his purpose" (KJV).

Life is not perfect. We have to deal with it as it is, but making up our minds to stay with God will change our lives forever. I've been leading God's people for 16 years now and I've never felt like giving up on God. He is the one who made us, and He only wants us to do His will. I never had to find God.

He was always there in plain sight, but I was too deep in my own way to stop and acknowledge His presence and person.

Yes, when I got saved, then all hell broke loose. I became unstable. Maybe so I could learn to solely depend on Him. Bad things just kept happening, especially my living arrangements. I couldn't understand how I could be so faithful, sincerely desiring to serve God, and be going through so much. In fact, when the Lord called me to be a pastor, I was sleeping on somebody's floor. I didn't have anywhere to live. I was actually staying with a member of my daughter's father's family. While staying at her home, that's when the Lord slowed me down. I was making things harder because I didn't think I was qualified to lead a congregation. I thought, "I don't have the education. I've never been to Bible College." The insecurities flooded my mind. I asked, "God, could you really use me? No, I don't think you want to do this."

I decided right then to start my church at that lady's house. I said, "God I'm going to do your work that you're calling me to do." I started the church right in the woman of God's house while she went to church. After the lady found out that I was having church in her house, she didn't feel good about it because she said I could've started going to church with her instead of having church in her house. I explained to her, saying, "Well, we are just having prayer, not really like church."

She was adamant and said, "Well, you know, you have to take it out of my house."

I knew this lady who had a little office space, and I asked

her if she could rent it to me. She said "yes" with no problem. I rented the space for $300 per month. During this time, I was working four hours a day in Deerfield Beach, which was like no money after buying food and paying for transportation. Still, I used the little money I was making, and I always paid as agreed each month for that place. I started out with only one young lady coming to service because the other lady who was joining us in the house stopped coming when I got the office space. So, it was just me, her and my two youngest children starting out initially. The one young lady remained faithful, and she stayed with me as the ministry grew. Even now, 16 years later and now having a church building, she is still with me.

While I was at my present church, the Lord spoke to me concerning prayer, so I was facilitating a huge intercessory prayer session each week. Eventually, I had to go to my leaders at church and ask them for permission to do a prayer group. They agreed to give me Thursday night. So, I was hosting this prayer service at my church once a week, and it was growing in size and popularity. A lot of people came to church talking about it, but then the pastor said he didn't think that I should host a prayer service that was outdoing the congregation on Sundays. I then asked the church leadership if I could take it to a hotel, and they agreed to that. So, then I moved the service to a local hotel. The prayer service got so huge that my pastor came to me again and said that I needed to bring it back to the church. I love to walk in obedience, so I took it back to the church again. After this second move, a lot of people were asking me, "Are you crazy? Why does the pastor keep telling you this and then that, and you're just doing everything that the pastor says?"

I explained, "If I walk in obedience, then God will do the rest." That said, I took the service back to the church. Again, it was huge group with lots of people coming for three weeks. By the fourth week, everything started out well but then started going down and down each week thereafter. It eventually went down to five people. Then my pastor said to me, "You know, Sonia, I think you should shut it down or take it back to the hotel."

I decided to go back to the hotel. Eventually, I stopped hosting the prayer service altogether because I didn't want it to become a situation where I would have to be asking for an offering or anything like that. I didn't want to get into any money business because I saw where it was getting a little bit shaky with me financially to keep paying to host it outside the church. I then hosted it at one of my friend's home one day per week. And after having it at her home, then I started to go from home to home so it wouldn't be a burden on one person. I did this for nearly five years before I ended up leaving that church. Prior to officially leaving, I wrote the pastor a letter and told him that "the Lord will have me to do His work." He said they didn't see where I was ready to lead a congregation. I simply said, "Okay," and gave them the letter. The leadership gave me their blessing, but I didn't start a church or anything like that immediately. Instead, I went to another church, and I helped that pastor for two years. Everything was going good with me because I know I heard from God. He was just telling me to do His work. So, I started to help the pastor and it worked out for about a year. Then after the next year, it was like déjà vu with the same back and forth with this pastor. She gave me Thursdays to do the prayer service in her church too. Then she said the prayer service was outdoing her church service and a lot of other things. So, I just said, "Alright, I need to take some time out and hear the Lord, and just seek the Lord for direction."

This is when I ended up staying with a close friend temporarily. I said, "I'm going to take some time out and seek the Lord because how can I go and start a church now and I don't have a real job? I have to pay for a place and everything like that." I didn't have any answers, but I was sure of the direction in which I had to walk.

I moved in this lady's house I didn't personally know. I was sleeping in a chair, and the chair broke one day and put me flat on the floor. I was staying there with my two youngest children, who didn't have anywhere to sleep other than the floor. Frustrated, I cried out, "God, I can't afford for you to do anything else." We were staying in the den of the lady's house. If she fried chicken, me and my kids would smell like chicken. We had to sleep on the floor in the den for a long time. I said, "Alright, God, if you're putting me on the floor, there's no further down for me to go. I'm gonna do your work." He heard me and that is how I started to work of the Lord. I never went back down. I started having service in the office space, and I got a bigger space as the congregation grew. As time went on, I had to get a bigger space and then a space larger than that. Today, here I am.

When I wasn't even driving, God blessed me with a car. Someone in church gave me a Toyota Camry. I was praying for this lady who came to the altar for prayer, so I went behind her to lay my hand on her back as I prayed. I didn't know that she was having back problems. After service, she told me about her back issues and she said that something "strange" happened to her. She said the Holy Spirit told her to give me that car. She was surprised because she said, "I just put four new tires on it."

_ I smiled and said, "Well, sweetheart, go back to the Holy Spirit. There's nothing that I can do."

I didn't hear from her for three days, but then I got a call and she said, "Sister Sonia, please come get this car out of my garage!"

I couldn't drive at the time because I didn't even have a learner's permit yet, so I got a young man from the church to go with me to go get the car. It stayed parked for about eight months before I could actually drive it myself. After prayer service on Thursday night, I had another member give me a fairly new Nissan Quest minivan. God was really making provisions.

Sometimes when I sit and think, how, God really brought me through all of this, tears come to my eyes because I could remember that one time I was just so isolated. I didn't have anybody to say, "You're doing good," for instance. People would come to the church and say things like, "I heard that you're sleeping on the floor. We don't want a pastor that's sleeping on the floor."

I went through it. I said, "God, if nobody proves you, I'm gonna prove you. I'm gonna know you for myself." God has blessed me, but not because of anything special I've done. He has blessed me in spite of what I have done. I found Him and He was guiding and protecting me even when I didn't know it. I kept believing God that if He called me, He would qualify me to do His work. Here I am today still leading God's people and becoming a teacher of His word. There is no better dream that I would've wanted to accomplish. I have gotten to a place in God where I can look back on the past and thank God for the process. I ended up in a nice building. I thank God for my covering: Apostle John L. Mohorn. He is truly a humble, decent man of God. He covers a lot of churches and been in ministry for 35 years. My church is under his covering.

Apostle Mohorn was the first one who prophesied to me saying, "God is going to have you to pastor his people." At that time, I was like three years in my walk with the Lord. I first met him when I went to a prayer service with a ministry friend before she was a pastor. I was in the audience and this man of God picked me out of the crowd and said, "God is going to have you to pastor His people." I've never saw him again until one day since having my own ministry, my spiritual son, a young man that I counsel, came all the way from Atlanta, Georgia, to visit me. He was hosting a service at a local church and invited me to attend. When I arrived and got out my car, I noticed a familiar faced as I walked inside. It was clearly Apostle Mohorn. I shouted, "Oh, my God! Oh, my god! I met you so many years ago, and you prophesied to me."

He said, "Are you pastoring a church now? Are you doing the work of the Lord?"

Excitedly, I said, "Yes, sir."

"Okay," he responded.

At that time, I never thought about asking him to be the covering over my ministry. I just kept praying and seeking the Lord. We were doing fine at the church, but I knew in my heart that I needed the accountability and oversight. One day, nearly a year later, I was in my bed and Apostle Mohorn just came up in front of me. Immediately, I thought, "I think he is going to be my covering. I think I need him to be my covering."

About three days after that premonition, my oldest daughter, Dorrette, who works at the courthouse called me and said, "Mommy, after prayer with the ladies at the courthouse, the Lord definitely spoke to me." She said, "Mommy, I'm serious. You know who the Lord showed me as your covering?"

I said, "Who?"

She said, "Apostle Mohorn."

"What?" I replied in shock.

"Yeah," she said.

That call was the great confirmation of covering for this man of God who would become a close friend, spiritual father and wise counselor for the church. The name of the ministry that God gave me is "Heart of Compassion Ministry." We are built on love and unity. I do believe that it doesn't matter what denomination you represent. I have learned to accept people for who they are and let God do the rest. So, our motto is: "Where everybody is somebody in Jesus name."

As a pastor I strive to be different. Coming from the streets, there are a lot of lessons that I've learned. One of them is I don't think that you are better than me and vice versa. I'm not that pastor who had her mother or father serve as pastor. Even though I grew up in the church, I was out there in the world. So, when I see someone that comes to the church who is a babe in Christ, I'm extra patient. I cannot look down on people because they can't understand living purely under God's grace. They will have to learn to experience God from an obedience standpoint. I cannot make them do that because here I am reborn again by grace through faith, not of my own doing. To be honest, I'm just happy they're coming to church and seeking, in any small way, God's attention. However, at the same time, it's all about making up your mind, knowing that you want to serve God. It was still on me, and it's ultimately all up to them. I had already made up my mind when God called me to ministry. It was my time to come and I came. Unsaved members will likewise come to God too when it's time. Only God knows the heart (Jeremiah 17:10) and when those who have not yet come to know Him will decide to trust Him with their life. Meanwhile, we should not judge; we should pray. God knew the reason He called me because I was a wretched sinner. I was out there being a problem and causing problems. God calling me was like winning a gold medal. I said I will not hurt His feelings. I will not disappoint Him. Those kinds of thoughts and feelings about salvation made me more determined. So that's the determination that I come to God with, because I know, if it had not been for him, I would be behind bars or probably six feet under. But by His grace and mercy, and I do believe in the power of a praying mother, the Lord turned my life around. I'm so excited about my salvation, so I can't look down on people. Instead, I show them love. I encourage them. I say, "There is greatness on the inside of you, and the Lord can use you." All those great encouragements are genuine and do work.

I have a lot of young people in my ministry, and they keep me going. For instance, I have some devoted young praise dancers, and I travel with them. Dancing unto God, they have a unique outlet for praise and worship. To see God delivering, healing and anointing people is truly miraculous, and it is why I stay inspired to keep going. I know that. If God can transform me, he can change anyone. The Lord said to me, "Sonia, don't look for perfect people. Look for people who are available." Because most perfect people that think they're perfect and are not available to be used by God. That's how God deals with me.

So those young girls have to be in Sunday school. That's number one. They have to be present at church. They have to be in Bible study and they also have to be in intercessory prayer. The reason for that is it teaches them commitment, and I told them, "Listen, you guys, you're ministers, so you got to be clean." I've learned that when the Holy Spirit comes in, we have to keep it clean, for without it, we have no revelation of the word of God. We often battle with two spirits: the Holy Spirit and unclean spirits. God always give us a way of escape, though. You have to live the best way you can.

I have a lot of young people, and I make sure they do something in ministry. For instance, I let them usher, but I have older people as well. What is happening is that young people are coming from the streets, and they usually go to the club or go out partying. Thus, I try to keep them busy in positive ministry activities. They go to the movies, and there's nothing wrong with going to the movies or having fun when they go their different ways. So, when they come into the church, I cannot close them off completely from the world like that. I try to keep them busy. I have a few of them who have gotten married. It's just so good with these young girls, and I really give God thanks for them.

In the ministry that I have, the young people are not bored. They serve in the ministry, but they have balance. I planned various outings and vacations so that they can enjoy fellowshipping with each other. As a believer, you can enjoy yourselves and love the Lord. I truly believe people must be free. I don't think they must be forced into serving God. I think because forcing someone against their will or desire will eventually result in a negative attitude toward religion or even God. Furthermore, some may rebel.

Seeking and following the will of God is what will make the ultimate difference in our lives, but oftentimes, our human will always wants to present itself in conflict with God's. If we resist and persist, God will give us the victory over all temptation and unrighteousness. The Bible in James 4:7 says: "Submit yourselves therefore to God. Resist the devil, and he will flee from you" (KJV). In living for God, we must obey His commandments, and one of the most evident is His heart's desire that we should give to the less fortunate. As it says in Proverbs 31:20, "She opens her hand to the poor and reaches out her hands to the needy." I enjoy feeding the homeless because I understand their plight. I'm active with young people but I'm also very active in the community. We support the community through the year. It doesn't have to be a special occasion or holiday to feed the poor. Some churches do it for Thanksgiving, I do it whenever or with whatever I have. As soon as I get the food, I take it to the community. I have another church that always support me with food. We are packaging it up and handing it out. When we get stuff from other companies too, we just give it to the community as well. We also help other pastors that pack supplies and send them to different countries.

In general, I love to help people. I used to go out and decorate people's home. I will go shop for them if necessary because I love to decorate the places. I think the way ministry is actively expressed in me is giving and helping. That's my happy place. Once I can help, I'm good.

Everything is thriving now. I got healing from my past. I told my kids about the rape one Christmas and we all cried together. My life is much better. It's way better because going through difficult times, I do believe that it's also built my faith, especially those times we were homeless and God provided. There's a lot of things that I still do not understand, but I always trust God despite what I see. Growing up and seeing my mother struggle, I now understand because I saw that she came out as pure gold. On my side, I understand, but on the side of my children, they couldn't understand why I was unable to make provision for them. You know why I can't have a stable place for them to live. God has put us together and we are all stable now. My ministry is more grounded. I've been in this building for nearly 12 years. There has been a lot of growth. It's very much stable than before.

This is a legacy. I am gifted in many things. I'm a great cook and always wanted to have a restaurant. But since I came to the Lord and came into pastoral leadership, I put a lot of natural aspirations away. I put them down; I didn't cancel them until God tells me otherwise. Recently for instance, one of my daughters called me and said, "Let's do a business." So, we have started multiple businesses, and God is blessing our efforts. Most importantly, I know that my children will carry on this legacy because the Word of the Lord never fails.

Final Word

I have discovered my true identity in God. There is no way you can discover your true identity, without God coming into your life, which makes you *become a new creature, old things have passed away and behold all things become new* (2 Corinthians 5:17). And the true you will be revealed.

Getting to this point in my life did not come easy, but it was worth it. I walked through a period of my life where I was talked about, lied on, told I would never make it, that my children would never come out to anything, that I would not last in ministry, and that I was not qualified to lead God's people. The enemy speaks so loud that you have to know that you know, that the Creator is who He said that He is. I choose life with God now and forever, and making this decision has not been easy. Nevertheless, I choose this road anyway. The problem with us is that we choose life and refuse to stay connected with the One who gives it. Leaving my kids and constantly moving around was never easy, but I felt like I was making a sacrifice for them at the time. I'm so happy and blessed that I chose the right path, and God stepped in to be everything to them that I couldn't be. To God be the glory for the great things He has done in my life. I have no regrets knowing that *the just shall live my faith* and not by sight (Habakkuk 2:4, Romans 1:17, Galatians 2:16), and that *the race is not for the swift nor the strong, but it is for those who will endure to the end* (Ecclesiastes 9:11).

Hopefully, the happiness that I found in God has encouraged you as you read this book, knowing that repentance is not merely a sad feeling, but rather a heartfelt decision to change, which I did. Given that decision, I had to develop a relationship with God by getting into the His word, seeking His will, and choosing His ways. This is the roadmap that led me to my destiny. The Lord never promised me or anyone that road was going to be easy. However, He promised to *never leave us nor forsake us*, and He will be with us until the end (Deuteronomy 31:6). Cherish that thought, and know that we are never alone.

www.ingramcontent.com/pod-product-compliance
Lightning Source LLC
Chambersburg PA
CBHW060351130626
46553CB00003B/1180